Keto Air Fryer Cookbook
Easy and Healthy Low Carb Recipes
You'll Want to Try ASAP

Brandon Hearn© 2018

D1374267

Table of Contents

Introduction

If you're on the ketogenic diet, you already know that sticking to your new lifestyle is essential in your success if you want to stay in ketosis and reap the benefits. Your air fryer can help you do this. Let's start with some air fryer basics. It's a kitchen appliance that's easy to use, and it cooks your food by circulating hot air around it. It's powered using mechanical fans, which you can increase the temperature of depending on what you're trying to cook. It allows for a crispy finish too!

The best part is that it only requires a few drops of oil. With the ketogenic diet, you use a lot of healthy oil, but these oils can't be cooked at high temperatures often. For example, olive oil is great for salad, but it's not great for deep frying. They're an affordable kitchen appliance that will fit any household. Luckily, it doesn't require a lot of maintenance either!

When you're switching over to the ketogenic diet, giving up your comfort food can be something that's extremely difficult. It'll leave you with cravings that make you feel low when you aren't satisfying them. You want unhealthy, crispy food.

You may caramelized onions or curry that you can't quite have on the keto diet. The air fryer can help you to cook a healthy, ketogenic friendly version of your favorite foods. You can get crispy fried food without the high carbs and without the high calories. If you like 'breading' on your food, then the ketogenic diet becomes extremely difficult to follow without an air fryer instead, you'll want to finely chop nuts and seeds to give it a similar coating.

Believe it or not the air fryer isn't just for fried food either. You can use it for breakfast, lunch, dinner, snacks, side dishes and even desserts. You can create delicious meals at home, and it makes meals quickly. Since it uses hot air to cook your food it shortens the cooking time. All of your flavors will stay in the cooker too, since it won't be evaporating out of the pan. Most air fryers even come with a heating option so that you can reheat your food if you have leftovers too without losing that crunch.

You can get healthy desserts from an air fryer that are keto friendly too. You can even cook cookies in your air fryer. Just because you're on a diet doesn't mean you have to completely deny your sweet tooth. Believe it or not, you can even make pudding in our air fryer.

Air Fryer Components

If you're completely new to the air fryer, you're going to need to understand the components to use it properly. Here's an easy breakdown of your air fryer.

- **Cooking Chamber:** This is where the actual cooking takes place. What it actually looks like will vary depending on your brand. Some have racks, others have normal cooking baskets, and some have walled cook baskets. No matter what air fryer you get, it should be compatible with each of these recipes. Some brands are just known to be more durable than others.

- **Heating Element:** This is the coil inside of your fryer, and it produces the heat using the electricity passing through it. Once it reaches the temperature you want, the air is pushed through the coil, and it heats up as it passes the fan and grill.

- **Fan & Grill:** This is the part that actually cooks your food at the bottom of your air fryer. They're responsible for circulation and keeping the air superheated to get the crispness on your food.

- **Exhaust System:** This helps to get rid of harmful buildup of excess pressure. Most modern air fryers include filters as well, which will help you to get rid of unpleasant odors and dirt that may get into your air fryer so that they don't affect your food.

- **Food Tray:** These are usually transferable, but there are some brands that have boundary walls built in the try, allowing you to cook multiple dishes. This tray will vary depending on the air fryer you get, so make sure that you get a tray that work for how you'll be using your air fryer the most. For example, you may want one that has s universal handle, which makes removing it from the heating chamber easy.

Keto Air Fryer Tips

The ketogenic diet is easy with the air fryer, but we'll make it even easier with these keto air fryer tips.

Use Keto Oils

Remember that you're on the ketogenic diet, so you need to make sure that you're using keto friendly oils. You'll need to use either olive oil or coconut oil depending on the recipe. Butter is also an oil that you can use to cook. Make sure to stay away from vegetable and canola oil whenever possible.

Make Sure to Preheat It

You'll need to preheat your air fryer at least most of the time. Make sure to check your recipe, but most will tell you to heat it up first so that you don't cook your food before it's hot enough to really crisp it. Your food will still turn out delicious if you forget to preheat it, but you won't have the texture that the air fryer is known for if you forget.

Grease Your Basket

You'll need to grease your basket if you don't want your food to stip. Even if you're coating your food in oil, it sometimes needs greased to make sure that the "breading" stays in place. Always follow your recipe, but have your greasing agent ready to go at the beginning of your recipes. Remember not to use aerosol sprays for your air fryer either. Many of these sprays, such as Pam, can cause chipping in some baskets, so it's best not to use them.

Reduce Calories & Carbs

Your air fryer allows you to reduce your calories and carbs naturally. After all, you'll have less oil and therefore less calories. The ketogenic friendly recipes will help to make sure that you clearly know the calories and net carbs that you're taking in. most people can have up to 23 net carbs a day, but you may need to adjust your calorie intake as well. Listen to your body and keep a food journal of both your net carbs and your calories per day so you know if you're meeting your health goals.

Wait a Half Hour

Before you clean your air fryer, you'll need to wait a half hour after your turn off your air fryer to make sure that it's completely cool. Remember that even if you open your air fryer during cooking, it's designed to make sure that it doesn't cool down too easily. For that reason, you have to give it adequate cooling time if you don't want to hurt yourself.

Pay Attention to Portions

When you're cooking most or all of your meal in an air fryer, it becomes easier to pay attention to the portions you're eating. It's easy to over fill a pan, but it's not nearly as easy to over fill an air fryer because it wouldn't cook properly. Pay attention to how much you're putting into your air fryer, and make sure that you can divide it up evenly so that your food gets the texture it needs, and it'll make sure that you don't go over your allotted net carbs either.

Breakfast Recipes

Breakfast is easy with your air fryer even on the ketogenic diet! You can even cook porridge in your air fryer.

Avocado Boats

Serves: 2 **Time:** 18 Minutes
Calories: 288 **Protein:** 7.6 Grams
Fat: 26 Grams **Net Carbs:** 6 Grams
Ingredients:
- 2 Eggs
- 1 Avocado, Halved & Pitted
- Fresh Chives, Chopped
- Fresh Parsley, Chopped
- Salt & Pepper to Taste

Directions:
1. Start by scooping out some flesh from your avocado, and season what's left with chives, parsley, salt and pepper.
2. Crack one egg into each half, and then place them in your air fryer basket.
3. Cook at 350 for six minutes.
4. Serve with more chives.

Easy Frittata

Serves: 6 **Time:** 25 Minutes
Calories: 202 **Protein:** 15.1 Grams
Fat: 15 Grams **Net Carbs:** 2.7 Grams
Ingredients:

- 6 Eggs
- ½ Onion
- 1 Tomato
- 1/3 Cup Heavy Cream
- 1 Teaspoon Sea Salt, Fine
- 1 Tablespoon Butter
- 1 Tablespoon Oregano
- 6 Ounces Parmesan
- 1 Teaspoon Chili Powder

Directions:

1. Crack your eggs into your air fryer basket, and whisk gently.
2. Add in your diced onion and chopped tomato.
3. Add your vegetables, and then pour in your heavy cream.
4. Sprinkle with butter, oregano, chili pepper and salt.
5. Add in shredded parmesan, and then heat your air fryer to 375.
6. Cook for fifteen minutes, and serve warm.

Egg Soufflé

Serves: 2 **Time:** 18 Minutes
Calories: 116 **Protein:** 5.9 Grams
Fat: 9.9 Grams **Net carbs:** 0.8 Grams
Ingredients:

- 2 Eggs
- 2 Tablespoons Heavy Cream
- ¼ Teaspoon Ground Chili Pepper
- 1 Tablespoon Parsley
- ¼ Teaspoon Sea Salt, Fine

Directions:

1. Start by preheating your air fryer to 391, and then get out a bowl.

2. Crack your eggs, and mix in your heavy cream, whisking well.

3. Sprinkle in your parsley, salt and chili pepper.

4. Spoon the mixture into two ramekins, and cook for eight minutes.

5. Allow it to chill for two to three minutes before serving.

Coconut Porridge

Serves: 4 **Time:** 18 Minutes
Calories: 279 **Protein:** 5.7 Grams
Fat: 24.6 Grams **Net Carbs:** 4.2 Grams
Ingredients:

- 1 Teaspoon Cinnamon
- 5 Tablespoons Chia Seeds
- 1 Cup Coconut Milk
- ¼ Teaspoon Sea Salt, Fine
- 3 Tablespoons Blackberries
- 3 Tablespoons Coconut Flakes
- 1 Teaspoon Butter
- 2 Tablespoons Walnuts

Directions:

1. Pour your coconut milk into your tray, and then add in your cinnamon, butter, chia seeds, salt and coconut flakes.
2. Crush your walnuts before adding them in to, and then sprinkle your salt over the mixture.
3. Mash your blackberries gently, placing them into your basket too.
4. Heat your air fryer to 375, and cook for seven minutes.
5. Remove it from the air fryer, allowing it to rest for five minutes before serving.

Spinach Quiche

Serves: 6
Time: 36 Minutes
Calories: 248
Protein: 12.8 Grams
Fat: 20.2 Grams
Net Carbs: 2.7 Grams
Ingredients:

- 4 Tablespoons Water, Boiled
- ½ Cup Almond Flour
- 1 Cup Spinach
- 1 Teaspoon Sea Salt, Fine
- ¼ Cup Cream Cheese
- ½ Onion
- 1 Teaspoon Black Pepper
- 6 Ounces Cheddar Cheese, Shredded
- 3 Eggs
- 1 Teaspoon Olive Oil

Directions:

1. Combine your almond flour, water and salt. Mix until it forms a soft dough. It shouldn't be sticky.

2. Spray your air fryer down with olive oil, and preheat it to 375.
3. Roll your dough out, placing it into your air fryer. It should be in the shape of a crust.
4. Cook for five minutes.
5. Chop your spinach, adding in your cream cheese and black pepper.
6. Add in your diced onion, stirring well.
7. Get out a bowl and beat your eggs well.
8. Transfer the spinach filling into your crust, and then sprinkle with cheese. Pour your eggs over it, and then cook at 350 for seven minutes.
9. Reduce your air fryer's heat to 300, and then cook for nine minutes more.
10. Allow it to cool before slicing to serve.

Pancake Hash

Serves: 7 **Time:** 18 Minutes
Calories: 178 **Protein:** 4.4 Grams
Fat: 13.3 Grams **Net Carbs:** 10.7 Grams
Ingredients:
- 1 Teaspoon Baking Soda
- 1 Tablespoon Apple Cider Vinegar
- 1 Teaspoon Sea Salt, Fine
- 1 Teaspoon Ginger
- 1 Cup Coconut Flour
- 5 Tablespoons Butter
- ¼ Cup Heavy Cream
- 1 Egg

Directions:
1. Get out a bowl and combine your salt ground ginger, flour and baking soda.
2. Get out another bowl, cracking your eggs into it, and then add in your heavy cream and butter.
3. Mix the liquid mixture well, and then add it to the dry mixture. Stir to combine.
4. Heat your air fryer to 400, and then pour the mixture into your basket.
5. Cook for four minutes, and then scramble. Cook for another five minutes.

Sweet Flax Meal Porridge

Serves: 4
Time: 15 Minutes
Calories: 298
Protein: 6.2 Grams
Fat: 26.7 Grams
Net Carbs: 3.9 Grams
Ingredients:

- ½ Teaspoon Vanilla Extract
- 1 Tablespoon Butter
- 1 Teaspoon Stevia
- 3 Tablespoons Flax Meal
- 1 Cup Almond Milk
- 2 Tablespoons Sesame Seeds
- 4 Tablespoons Chia Seeds

Directions:

1. Preheat your air fryer to 375.

2. Place your chia seeds, sesame seeds, flax meal, almond milk, butter and stevia into your tray. Add in your vanilla, and then cook for eight minutes.

3. Stir well, and allow it to sit for five minutes before serving.

Cheddar Soufflé

Serves: 4
Time: 20 Minutes
Calories: 244
Protein: 13.5 Grams
Fat: 20.6 Grams
Net Carbs: 1.5 Grams
Ingredients:

- 4 Tablespoons Heavy Cream
- 1 Tablespoon Chives
- 1 Tablespoon Dill
- 1 Teaspoon Parsley
- ½ Teaspoon Thyme
- 3 Eggs
- 5 Ounces Cheddar Cheese, Shredded

Directions:

1. Get out a bowl, cracking your eggs into it. Whisk well, and then add in your heavy cream. Whisk for another ten seconds.
2. Add in your parsley, dill, chives and thyme.
3. Sprinkle your mixture with cheese before stirring again.
4. Pour into four ramekins, and then preheat your air fryer to 390. Place your ramekins in the air fryer, cooking for eight minutes.
5. Chill before serving.

Zucchini Breakfast Hash

Serves: 4 **Time:** 12 Minutes
Calories: 445 **Protein:** 26.3 Grams
Fat: 36.1 Grams **Net Carbs:** 2.5 Grams
Ingredients:

- 2 Tablespoons Butter
- 7 Ounces Bacon, Cooked
- 1 Zucchini
- 4 Ounces Cheddar Cheese
- 2 Tablespoons Butter
- 1 Teaspoon Sea Salt, Fine
- 1 Teaspoon Black Pepper
- 1 Teaspoon Cilantro
- 1 Teaspoon Thyme, Ground
- 1 Teaspoon Paprika

Directions:

1. Cube your zucchini, and sprinkle it with cilantro, pepper, salt, paprika and them.
2. Preheat your air fryer to 400, and toss your butter into the tray.
3. Allow it to melt before adding in your zucchini, cooking for five minutes.
4. Shred your cheddar, and shake your zucchini cubes. Add in your bacon, and then add in your cheese. Cook for three more minutes.
5. Serve warm.

Bacon Scrambled Eggs

Serves: 4
Time: 20 Minutes
Calories: 387
Protein: 21.9 Grams
Fat: 32.1 Grams
Net Carbs: 1.9 Grams
Ingredients:

- ½ Teaspoon Nutmeg
- 1 Teaspoon Paprika
- 1 Tablespoon Butter
- 5 Tablespoons Heavy Cream
- 6 Ounces Bacon
- 4 Eggs
- 1 Teaspoon Sea Salt, Fine
- 1 Teaspoon Black Pepper

Directions:
1. Start by chopping your bacon small, and then sprinkle it with salt.
2. Stir your bacon, and then put it in an air fryer.
3. Preheat your air fryer to 360, and then add your bacon in. cook for five minutes.
4. Beat your eggs in a bowl, whisking well.
5. Sprinkle your egg mixture with pepper, nutmeg and paprika. Whisk well.
6. Toss your butter and egg mixture into your bacon and then add in your heavy cream. Cook for two more minutes.

7. Scramble your eggs cooking for three more minutes, and serve warm.

Tofu Scramble

Serves: 5
Time: 35 Minutes
Calories: 109
Protein: 11.2 Grams
Fat: 6.7 Grams
Net Carb: 1.5 Grams
Ingredients:

- 2 Eggs
- 10 Ounces Tofu Cheese
- 1 Teaspoon Chives
- 1 Tablespoon Apple Cider Vinegar
- ½ Teaspoon Sea Salt, Fine
- ¼ Teaspoon Coriander
- 1 Teaspoon White Pepper

Directions:

1. Start by shredding your tofu cheese, sprinkling it with salt, apple cider vinegar, white pepper and coriander.
2. Mix it up, allowing it to marinate for ten minutes.
3. Heat your air fryer to 370, and then add in your tofu cheese. Cook for thirteen minutes.
4. Beat your eggs in a bowl, whisking well.
5. Pour your egg mixture over your shredded tofu cheese, and then stir using a spatula.
6. When your eggs are beginning to firm cook for seven minutes more, and then serve warm.

Hemp Porridge

Serves: 3 **Time:** 25 Minutes
Calories; 196 **Protein:** 5.1 Grams
Fat: 18.2 Grams **Net Carbs:** 1.8 Grams
Ingredients:
- 2 Tablespoons Flax Seeds
- 4 Tablespoon Hemp Seeds
- 1 Tablespoon Butter
- ¼ Teaspoon Sea Salt, Fine
- 1 Teaspoon Stevia
- ½ Teaspoon Ginger
- 7 Tablespoons Almond Milk

Directions:
1. Start by putting your hemp and flax seeds in the air fryer. Sprinkle with ginger and salt.
2. Combine your stevia and milk together, pouring it over your seeds before adding butter.
3. Preheat your air fryer to 370, and cook for fifteen minutes.
4. Stir well after ten minutes.
5. Allow it to chill for three minutes before serving.

Cloud Eggs

Serves: 2 **Time:** 12 Minutes
Calories: 80 **Protein:** 5.6 Grams
Fat: 6.3 Grams **Net Carbs:** 0.3 Grams
Ingredients:
- 1 Teaspoon Butter
- 2 Eggs

Directions:
1. Start by separating your egg whites from your yolks.

2. Start by whisking the egg yolks until you get stiff white peaks.

3. Spread the air fryer basket with butter, and then preheat it to 300. Place the gg whites in the basket, and then cook for two minutes.

4. Remove, and then place the yolks in the center of your clouds, and then cook for two more minutes. Serve warm.

Bacon & Egg Cups

Serves: 2 **Time:** 25 Minutes
Calories: 553 **Protein:** 37.3 Grams
Fat: 43.3 Grams **Net Carbs:** 1.9 Grams
Ingredients:

- ½ Teaspoon Butter
- 4 Ounces Bacon
- 2 Eggs
- ¼ Teaspoon Sea Salt, Fine
- ½ Teaspoon Butter
- 3 Ounces Cheddar Cheese, Shredded
- ½ Teaspoon Cayenne Pepper
- 1 Tablespoon Chives
- ½ Teaspoon Paprika

Directions:
1. Start by chopping your bacon into small pieces, sprinkling them with cayenne pepper, paprika and salt.
2. Mix well, and then spread them in ramekins with butter, beating your eggs in. add in your shredded cheese and chives.
3. Heat your air fryer to 360, placing your ramekins in.
4. Cook of twelve minutes, and allow them to cool before serving.

Lunch Recipes

Lunch doesn't have to be hard either. Many of these recipes you're even able to take on the go.

Meaty Egg Rolls

Serves: 6 **Time:** 25 Minutes
Calories: 150 **Protein:** 13 Grams
Fat: 9.6 Grams **Net Carbs:** 1.3 Grams
Ingredients:
- ½ Cup Almond Flour
- 1 Teaspoon Sea Salt, Fine
- ¼ Cup Water
- 7 Ounces Ground Beef
- 1 Egg
- 1 Teaspoon Paprika
- 1 Teaspoon Black Pepper
- 1 Tablespoon Olive Oil

Directions:

1. Preheat your water until it boils, and then get out your almond flour and sea salt. Mix it in a bowl.

2. Add in your boiling water, and mix well. Knead into a soft dough, and then set it to the side.

3. Combine your ground beef, black pepper and paprika, mixing well.

4. Roast your meat for five minutes on medium heat, stirring frequently using a saucepan. Beat your egg in.

5. Cook your ground beef for four minutes, and then roll the dough out. Cut it into six squares.

6. Put your ground beef in each square, and then roll them into sticks.

7. Sprinkle with olive oil, and preheat your air fryer to 350.

8. Cook for eight minutes.

Ham Hash

Serves: 3
Time: 20 Minutes
Calories: 372
Protein: 33.2 Grams
Fat: 23.7 Grams
Net Carbs: 5.9 Grams
Ingredients:

- 5 Ounces Parmesan
- 10 Ounces Ham
- 1 Teaspoon Black Pepper
- 1 Teaspoon Paprika
- 1 Egg
- ½ Onion
- 1 Tablespoon Butter

Directions:

1. Start by shredding your parmesan, and then slice your ham into strips.
2. Peel your onion before dicing it, and then crack your egg open in a bowl. Whisk well, and then add in your butter, diced onions, and ham strips.
3. Sprinkle this mixture with paprika and black pepper.
4. Mix well, and heat your air fryer to 350.
5. Transfer this mixture into three separate ramekins, sprinkling with parmesan.
6. Make sure to preheat your air fryer, and cook for ten minutes. Serve warm.

Pork Fried Rice

Serves: 3 **Time:** 20 Minutes
Calories: 376 **Protein:** 34 Grams
Fat: 33 Grams **Net Carbs:** 9.6 Grams
Ingredients:
- 2 Eggs
- 2 Cloves Garlic, Chopped
- ½ Cauliflower Head, Medium
- 3 Green Capsicums, Mini
- 2 Cups Pork Belly
- 2 Onions
- 1 Teaspoon Black Sesame Seeds
- 1 Teaspoon Picked Ginger
- 1 Tablespoon Soy Sauce

Directions:
1. Start by chopping your cauliflower to make small florets.
2. Get out a food processor, placing your cauliflower inside, and pulse until you get cauliflower rice.
3. Preheat your air fryer to 400, and then grease down your basket.
4. Beat your eggs, and then swirl them into your air fryer. Allow them to cook for five minutes, turning it down to 350.
5. Add in your cauliflower rice and pork next before tossing in your soy sauce and onion. Cook for another ten minutes at 375.
6. Garnish with picked ginger and sesame seeds.

Ketogenic Mac & Cheese

Serves: 4 **Time:** 20 Minutes
Calories: 135.5 **Protein:** 27 Grams
Fat: 10.2 Grams **Net Carbs:** 1.4 Grams
Ingredients:

- 3 Tablespoons Avocado Oil
- Sea Salt & Black Pepper to Taste
- 1 Cauliflower, Medium
- ¼ Cup Heavy Cream
- ¼ Cup Almond Milk, Unsweetened
- 1 Cup Cheddar Cheese, Shredded

Directions:

1. Start by preheating your air fryer to 400, and then make sure to grease your air fryer basket.
2. Chop your cauliflower into florets, and then drizzle oil over them. Toss until they're well coated, and then season with salt and pepper to taste.
3. Heat your cheddar, heavy cream, milk and avocado oil in a pot, pouring the mixture over your cauliflower.
4. Cook for fourteen minutes, and then serve warm.

Salmon Pie

Serves: 8 **Time:** 50 Minutes
Calories: 134 **Protein:** 13.2 Grams
Fat: 8.1 Grams **Net Carbs:** 2.2 Grams
Ingredients:

- 1 Teaspoon Paprika
- ½ Cup Cream
- ½ Teaspoons Baking Soda
- 1 ½ Cups Almond Flour
- 1 Onion, Diced
- 1 Tablespoon Apple Cider Vinegar
- 1 lb. Salmon
- 1 Tablespoon Chives
- 1 Teaspoon Dill
- 1 Teaspoon Oregano
- 1 Teaspoon Butter
- 1 Teaspoon Parsley
- 1 Egg

Directions:

1. Start by beating your eggs in a bowl, making sure they're whisked well. Add in your cream, whisking for another two minutes.

2. Add in your apple cider vinegar and baking soda, stirring well.

3. Add in your almond flour, combining until it makes a non-stick, smooth dough.

4. Chop your salmon into pieces, and then sprinkle your seasoning over it.

5. Mix well, and then cut your dough into two parts.

6. Place parchment paper over your air fryer basket tray, placing the first part of your dough in the tray to form a crust. Add in your salmon filling.

7. Roll out the second part, covering your salmon filling. Secure the edges, and then heat your air fryer to 360.

8. Cook for fifteen minutes, and then reduce the heat to 355, cooking for another fifteen minutes.

9. Slice and serve warm.

Garlic Chicken Stir

Serves: 4 **Time:** 25 Minutes
Calories: 275 **Protein:** 25.6 Grams
Fat: 15.7 Grams **Net Carbs:** 5.9 Grams
Ingredients:

- ½ Cup Coconut Milk
- ½ Cup Chicken Stock
- 2 Tablespoons Curry Paste
- 1 Tablespoon Lemongrass
- 1 Tablespoon Apple Cider Vinegar
- 2 Teaspoons Garlic, Minced
- 1 Onion
- 1 lb. Chicken Breast, Skinless & Boneless
- 1 Teaspoon Olive Oil

Directions:

1. Start by cubing your chicken, and then peel your onion before dicing it.
2. Combine your onion and chicken together in your air fryer basket, and then preheat it to 365. Cook for five minutes.
3. Add in your garlic, apple cider vinegar, coconut milk, lemongrass, curry paste and chicken stock. Mix well, and cook for ten minutes more.

4. Stir well before serving.

Chicken Stew

Serves: 6
Time: 30 Minutes
Calories: 102
Protein: 9.8 Grams
Fat: 4.5 Grams
Net Carbs: 4.1 Grams
Ingredients:

- 1 Teaspoon Cilantro
- 8 Ounces chicken Breast, Boneless & Skinless
- 1 Onion
- ½ Cup Spinach
- 2 Cups Chicken Stock
- 5 Ounces Cabbage
- 6 Ounces Cauliflower
- 1 Teaspoon Salt
- 1 Green Bell Pepper
- 1/3 Cup heavy Cream
- 1 Teaspoon Paprika
- 1 Teaspoon Butter
- 1 Teaspoon Cayenne Pepper

Directions:

1. Start by cubing your chicken breast, and then sprinkling your cilantro, cayenne, salt and paprika over it.
2. Heat your air fryer to 365, and then melt your butter in your air fryer basket.
3. Add your chicken cubes in, cooking it for four minutes.
4. Chop your spinach, and then dice your onion.
5. Shred your cabbage and cut your cauliflower into florets. Chop your green pepper next, and then add them into your air fryer.
6. Pour your chicken stock and heavy cream in, and then reduce your air fryer to 360. Cook for eight minutes, and stir before serving.

Goulash

Serves: 6
Time: 30 Minutes
Calories: 161
Protein: 20.3 Grams
Fat: 6.1 Grams
Net Carbs: 4.3 Grams
Ingredients:

- 1 White Onion
- 2 Green Peppers, Chopped
- 1 Teaspoon Olive Oil
- 14 Ounces Ground Chicken
- 2 Tomatoes
- ½ Cup Chicken Stock
- 1 Teaspoon Sea Salt, Fine
- 2 Cloves Garlic, Sliced
- 1 Teaspoon Black Pepper
- 1 Teaspoon Mustard

Directions:

1. Peel your onion before chopping it roughly.

2. Spray your air fryer down with olive oil before preheating it to 365.

3. Add in your chopped green pepper, cooking for five minutes.

4. Add your ground chicken and cubed tomato next. Mix well, and cook for six minutes.

5. Add in the chicken stock, salt, pepper, mustard and garlic. Mix well, and cook for six minutes more. Serve warm.

Beef & Broccoli

Serves: 4 **Time:** 25 Minutes
Calories: 187 **Protein:** 23.4 Grams
Fat: 7.3 Grams **Net Carbs:** 3.8 Grams
Ingredients:
- 1 Teaspoon Paprika
- 1 Onion
- 1/3 Cup Water
- 6 Ounces Broccoli
- 10 Ounces Beef Brisket
- 1 Teaspoon Canola Oil
- 1 Teaspoon Butter
- ½ Teaspoon Chili Flakes
- 1 Tablespoon Flax Seeds

Directions:
1. Start by chopping your beef brisket, and then sprinkle it with chili flakes and paprika. Mix your meat well, and then preheat your air fryer to 360.
2. Spray your air fryer down with canola oil, placing your beef in the basket tray. Cook for seven minutes, and make sure to stir once while cooking.
3. Chop your broccoli into florets, and then add them into your air fryer basket next.
4. Add in your butter and flax seeds before mixing in your water. Slice your onion, adding it into to, and stir well.

5. Cook at 265 for six minutes.
6. Serve warm.

Ground Beef Mash

Serves: 4 **Time:** 25 Minutes
Calories: 258 **Protein:** 35.5 Grams
Fat: 9.3 Grams **Net Carbs:** 4.9 Grams
Ingredients:

- 1 lb. Ground Beef
- 1 Onion
- 1 Teaspoon Garlic, Sliced
- ¼ Cup Cream
- 1 Teaspoon White Pepper
- 1 Teaspoon Olive Oil
- 1 Teaspoon Dill
- 2 Teaspoons Chicken Stock
- 2 Green Peppers
- 1 Teaspoon Cayenne Pepper

Directions:

1. Start by peeling your onion before grating it. Combine it with your sliced garlic, and then sprinkle your ground beef down with it. Add in your white pepper, and then add your cayenne and dill.

2. Coat your air fryer basket down with olive oil, heating it up to 365.

3. Place the spiced beef in the basket, cooking for three minutes before stirring. Add in the rest of your grated onion mixture and chicken stock, and then cook for two minutes more.

4. Chop your green peppers into small pieces, and then add them in.

5. Add in your cream, and stir well.

6. Allow it to cook for ten minutes more.

7. Mash your mixture to make sure it's scrambled before serving warm.

Chicken Casserole

Serves: 6 **Time:** 35 Minutes
Calories: 396 **Protein:** 30.4 Grams
Fat: 28.6 Grams **Net Carbs:** 2.8 Grams
Ingredients:

- 1 Tablespoon Butter
- 9 Ounces round Chicken
- ½ Onion
- 5 Ounces Bacon
- Sea Salt & Black Pepper to Taste
- 1 Teaspoon Turmeric
- 1 Teaspoon Paprika
- 6 Ounces Cheddar Cheese, Shredded
- 1 Egg
- ½ Cup Cream
- 1 Tablespoon Almond Flour

Directions:

1. Spread your butter into your air fryer tray, and then add in your ground chicken. Season with salt and pepper, and then add in your turmeric and paprika. Stir well, and then add in your cheddar cheese.
2. Beat your egg into your ground chicken, and mix well.
3. Whisk your cream and almond flour together.
4. Peel and dice your onion, and ten add it into your air fryer too.
5. Layer your cheese and bacon, and then heat your air fryer to 380.
6. Cook for eighteen minutes, and then allow it to cool slightly before serving.

Chicken Hash

Serves: 3 **Time:** 25 Minutes
Calories: 261 **Protein:** 21 Grams
Fat: 16.8 Grams **Net Carbs:** 4.4 Grams
Ingredients:
- 1 Tablespoon Water
- 1 Green Pepper
- ½ Onion
- 6 Ounces Cauliflower
- Chicken Fillet, 7 Ounces
- 1 Tablespoon cream
- 3 Tablespoon Butter
- Black Pepper to taste

Directions:
1. Start by roughly chopping your cauliflower before placing it in a blender. Blend until you get a cauliflower rice.
2. Chop your chicken into small pieces, and then get out your chicken fillets. Sprinkle with black pepper.
3. Heat your air fryer to 380, and then put your chicken in the air fryer basket. Add in your water and cream, cooking for six minutes.
4. Reduce the heat to 360, and then dice your green pepper and onion.
5. Add this to your cauliflower rice, and then add in your butter. Mix well, and then add it to your chicken. Cook for eight minutes.
6. Serve warm.

Snack Recipes

Yes, you can use your air fryer for snacks too! Many of these are great to serve for guests as well.

Cauliflower Fritters

Serves: 4 **Time:** 25 Minutes
Calories: 54 **Protein:** 3.3 Grams
Fat: 3.1 Grams **Net Carbs:** 2.7 Grams
Ingredients:
- 1 Teaspoon Sea Salt, Fine
- 1 Tablespoon Dill
- 1 Egg
- 10 Ounces Cauliflower
- 1 Teaspoon Olive Oil
- 1 Tablespoon Almond Flour
- 1 Tablespoon Parsley
- ½ Teaspoon White Pepper

Directions:

1. Rinse your cauliflower before chopping it. Make sure to chop it into small pieces, and then blend well.

2. Beat your egg before adding into your cauliflower, blending for another minute.

3. Transfer this to a bowl, sprinkling with almond flour, dill, salt, parsley and white pepper. Mix well, and then heat your air fryer to 355.

4. Sprinkle the basket with olive oil, and then place your fritters in the basket to fry.

5. Fry for eight minutes, and then turn them. Cook for another seven minutes. Serve warm.

Parmesan Sticks

Serves: 3 **Time:** 20 Minutes
Calories: 389 **Protein:** 28.6 Grams
Fat: 29.5 Grams **Net Carbs:** 4.4 Grams
Ingredients:

- ¼ Teaspoon Black Pepper
- 4 Tablespoons Almond Flour
- 1 Egg
- ½ Cup Heavy Cream
- 8 Ounces Parmesan Cheese

Directions:

1. Crack your egg into a bowl, beating it. Add in your almond flour and cream, mixing well.
2. Sprinkle your cream mixture with black pepper, whisking well.
3. Cut your cheese into short, thick sticks, and then dip it in the cream mixture. Place these sticks in a plastic bag and place them in the freezer. Let them freeze.
4. Turn your air fryer to 400, and then place your frozen sticks on the air fryer rack, and then cook for eight minutes.

Garlic Mozzarella Sticks

Serves: 4 **Time:** 1 Hour 15 Minutes
Calories: 80 **Protein:** 7 Grams
Fat: 6.2 Grams **Net Carbs:** 3 Grams
Ingredients:
- 1 Tablespoon Italian Seasoning
- 1 Cup Parmesan Cheese
- 8 Strings Cheeses, Diced
- 2 Eggs, Beaten
- 1 Clove Garlic, Minced

Directions:
1. Start by combining your parmesan, garlic and Italian seasoning in a bowl. Dip your cheese into the egg, and mix well.

2. Roll it into your cheese crumbles, and then press the crumbs into the cheese.

3. Place them in the fridge for an hour, and then preheat your air fryer to 375.

4. Spray your air fryer down with oil, and then arrange the cheese strings into the basket. Cook for eight to nine minutes at 365.

5. Allow them to cool for at least five minutes before serving.

Bacon Biscuits

Serves: 6 **Time:** 25 Minutes
Calories: 226 **Protein:** 9.2 Grams
Fat: 20.5 Grams **Net Carbs:** 1.2 Grams
Ingredients:

- 3 Tablespoons Butter
- 4 Tablespoons Heavy Cream
- 1 Teaspoon Oregano
- 1 Tablespoon Apple Cider Vinegar
- 1 Cup Almond Flour
- ½ Teaspoon Baking Soda
- 4 Ounces Bacon, Cooked
- 1 Egg

Directions:

1. Start by cracking your eggs in a bowl, whisking well.

2. Chop your bacon, adding it into your egg, sprinkling with apple cider vinegar and baking soda.

3. Add in your oregano and heavy cream, stirring well.

4. Add in your almond flour and butter next, and mix well.

5. Once your batter is smooth, and then preheat your air fryer to 400.

6. Pour your batter into muffin molds, and then cook for ten minutes.

7. Allow them to cool to room temperature before serving.

Zucchini Chips

Serves: 5
Time: 25 Minutes **Calories:** 22
Protein: 1 Gram **Fat:** 1.1 Grams
Net Carbs: 1.9 Grams
Ingredients:

- 2 Zucchini
- 1 Teaspoon Olive Oil
- 1 Teaspoon Paprika
- Sea Salt to Taste

Directions:

1. Preheat your air fryer to 370, and then slice your zucchini. Sprinkle your salt and paprika over the zucchini. Sprinkle them down with oil, and then cook for thirteen minutes.

Toasted Nuts

Serves: 4
Time: 15 Minutes
Calories: 230
Protein: 3.9 Grams
Fat: 23.9 Grams
Net Carbs: 1.5 Grams
Ingredients:

- ½ Cup Macadamia Nuts
- ½ Cup Pecans
- ¼ Cup Walnuts
- ¼ Cup Hazelnuts
- 1 Tablespoon Olive Oil
- 1 Teaspoon Sea Salt, Fine

Directions:

1. Start by turning your air fryer to 32, and then place your nuts in your air fryer.
2. Cook your nuts for eight minutes, and then stir. Cook for another four minutes.
3. Sprinkle them with oil and salt before shaking them. Cook for one more minute before serving.

Pork Bacon Bites

Serves: 6
Time: 30 Minutes
Calories: 239
Protein: 26.8 Grams
Fat: 13.7 Grams
Net Carbs: 2.6 Grams
Ingredients:

- 1 Teaspoon Olive Oil
- 1 Tablespoon Apple Cider Vinegar
- ½ Teaspoon Red Pepper
- 1 Teaspoon Turmeric
- 1 Teaspoon Sea Salt, Fine
- 1 lb. Pork Brisket
- 6 Ounces Bacon, Sliced

Directions:

1. Start by cutting your pork into bite size pieces, and then place your pork bites into a mixing bowl.
2. Sprinkle with red pepper, apple cider vinegar, turmeric and salt and mix well. Allow this to marinate for ten minutes, and then wrap each one in a slice of bacon. Secure them with toothpicks, and then heat your air fryer to 370.
3. Cook for eight minutes, and then flip them over. Cook for another six minutes. Allow them to cool down before serving.

Beef Jerky

Serves: 6 **Time:** 3 Hours
Calories: 129 **Protein:** 20.2 Grams
Fat: 4.1 Grams **Net Carb:** 0.9 Grams
Ingredients:

- 14 Ounces Beef Flank Steak
- 3 Tablespoons Apple Cider Vinegar
- 1 Teaspoon Chili Pepper
- 1 Teaspoon Black Pepper
- 1 Teaspoon Garlic Powder
- 1 Teaspoon Onion Powder
- ¼ Teaspoon Liquid Smoke

Directions:

1. Slice your beefsteak before tenderizing it.
2. Get out a bowl and combine your black pepper, onion powder, apple cider vinegar, garlic and liquid smoke.
3. Wisk well, and then transfer our beef into it. Stir well, and allow it to marinate for up eight hours. You have to at least let it marinate for ten minutes.
4. Cook your beef jerky at 150 for two and a half hours.
5. Allow it to cool before serving.

Chicken Poppers

Serves: 5 **Time:** 20 Minutes
Calories: 147 **Protein:** 15 Grams
Fat: 5.6 Grams **Net Carbs:** 3.7 Grams
Ingredients:

- 1 Teaspoon Garlic Powder
- 1 Teaspoon Black Pepper
- 1 Teaspoon Chili Flakes
- ½ Cup Coconut Flour
- 11 Ounces Chicken Breast, Boneless & Skinless
- 1 Tablespoon Canola Oil

Direction:

1. Start by cubing your chicken, and then place it in a bowl. Sprinkle your chicken cubes with black pepper, garlic, and chili flakes. Stir well, and then sprinkle your almond flour over it.

2. Sake the bowl so that the meat is coated properly, and preheat your air fryer to 365.

3. Sprinkle your air fryer down with your canola oil, and then cook your chicken for ten minutes.

4. Turn them over, cooking for another five minutes. Serve warm.

Pork Rinds

Serves: 8
Time: 18 Minutes
Calories: 329
Protein: 36.5 Grams
Fat: 20.8 Grams
Net Carbs: 0.1 Grams
Ingredients:
- ½ Teaspoon Black Pepper
- 1 Teaspoon Chili Flakes
- ½ Teaspoon Sea Salt, Fine
- 1 Teaspoon Olive Oil
- 1 lb. Pork Rinds

Directions:
1. Start by heating your air fryer to 365, and then spray it down with olive oil.

2. Place your pork rinds in your air fryer basket, and sprinkle with your seasoning. Mix well, and then cook for seven minutes.

3. Shake gently, and then serve cooled.

Chicken Skin Crisps

Serves: 6
Time: 16 Minutes
Calories: 350
Protein: 15.5 Grams
Fat: 31.4 Grams
Net Carbs: 0.1 Gram
Ingredients:

- 1 lb. Chicken Skin
- ½ Teaspoon Black Pepper
- 1 Teaspoon Dill
- ½ Teaspoon Chili Flakes
- 1 Teaspoon Butter
- ½ Teaspoon Sea Salt, Fine

Directions:

1. Slice your chicken skin roughly, and then sprinkle it with your seasoning.

2. Mix you're the chicken skin, and melt your butter before adding it.

3. Preheat your air fryer to 360, and then place your chicken skin in your air fryer basket.

4. Cook for three minutes per side, and then serve warm or room temperature.

Dinner Recipes

Dinner doesn't have to be hard. The air fryer helps you to cook meals and entrees in less time than standard cooking methods.

Coconut Cod Fritters

Serves: 8
Time: 25 Minutes
Calories: 348
Protein: 19.3 Grams
Fat: 27.4 Grams
Net Carbs: 3.5 Grams
Ingredients:

- ¼ Teaspoon Lemon Zest, Grated
- 2 Tablespoons Lemon Juice
- ½ Cup Cheddar Cheese, Grated
- ¼ Cup Coconut, Grated
- 1 lb. Cod Fillet
- 1 Tablespoon Parsley, Fresh & Chopped
- 2 Teaspoons Garlic, Minced
- 2 Teaspoons Paprika
- ¼ Cup Butter
- ½ Cup Mayonnaise

Directions:

1. Start by melting your butter in the microwave before allowing it to cool. Cube your cod, and then get out your food processor.

2. Add in your coconut, lemon juice, lemon zest, parsley, garlic and paprika. Pulse until smooth, and then add in your butter. Mix well, and then add in your cod. Pulse and form into fritters.

3. Turn your air fryer to 380, and then arrange your cod in the basket, cooking for six minutes. Flip them, and cook for six minutes more.

Catfish Nuggets

Serves: 6 **Time:** 30 Minutes
Calories: 140 **Protein:** 13.1 Grams
Fat: 8.7 Grams **Net Carbs:** 1.1 Grams
Ingredients:

- 1 lb. Catfish Fillet
- 1 Teaspoon Garlic, Minced
- 1 Egg, Large
- ½ Onion, Diced
- 1 Tablespoon Butter, Melted
- 1 Teaspoon Thyme, Ground
- 1 Teaspoon Coriander
- 1 Teaspoon Turmeric
- 1 Teaspoon Coriander
- ¼ Teaspoon Nutmeg
- 1 Teaspoon Flax Seeds

Directions:

1. Start by cutting your catfish into six bite size pieces, and then sprinkle them with garlic. Mix well.
2. Add in your remaining ingredients, making sure to coat it well.
3. Turn your air fryer to 360, and then melt your butter, spraying it over your catfish bites. Freeze your catfish nuggets.
4. Place them in the air fryer, cooking for sixteen minutes.

Chicken & Eggplant Lasagna

Serves: 8
Time: 40 Minutes
Calories: 348
Protein: 31.4 Grams
Fat: 20.6 Grams
Net Carbs: 5.6 Grams
Ingredients:

- 6 Ounces Cheddar Cheese, Shredded
- 7 Ounces Parmesan Cheese, Shredded
- 1 lb. Ground Chicken
- 2 Eggplants
- 1 Teaspoon Sea Salt, Fine
- 1 Teaspoon Paprika
- ½ Teaspoon Cayenne Pepper
- ½ Cup Heavy Cream
- 2 Teaspoons Butter
- 1 White Onion, Diced

Directions:

1. Spread your butter in your air fryer basket tray, and then peel and slice your eggplant.

2. Separate your eggplant into three even parts.

3. Mix your ground chicken with cayenne, salt, paprika and your diced onion, making sure to mix well. Separate this mixture into two equal parts.

4. Layer your air fryer with eggplant first, and then add a chicken later on top. Sprinkle with half of your cheddar cheese, and then layer on sliced eggplant again. Add another layer of ground chicken and the remainder of your cheddar cheese. Cover this layer with eggplants, and then add in your parmesan next.

5. Pour your butter and heavy cream in next, and then heat your air fryer to 365. Cook for seventeen minutes, and serve warm.

Southern Pulled Pork

Serves: 4 **Time:** 35 Minutes
Calories: 198 **Protein:** 30.7 Grams
Fat: 6.8 Grams **Net Carbs:** 1.8 Grams
Ingredients:

- ½ Teaspoon Paprika
- 1 Teaspoon Black Pepper
- 1 Tablespoon Chili Flakes
- 1 Teaspoon Cayenne Pepper
- 1/3 Cup Cream
- 1 lb. Pork Tenderloin
- 1 Teaspoon Sea Salt, Fine
- 4 Cups Chicken Stock
- 1 Teaspoon Thyme, Ground
- 1 Teaspoon Butter

Directions:

1. Place your chicken stock into your air fryer, and then get out your pork. Sprinkle it with black pepper, paprika, cayenne, salt and chili flakes.

2. Heat your air fryer to 370, and then cook for twenty minutes.

3. Strain your liquid, and then shred your meat.

4. Add your butter and cream to the mix, and then cook at 360 for four minutes.

5. Allow it to cool before serving.

Parmesan Beef

Serves: 4 **Time:** 40 Minutes
Calories: 348 **Protein:** 42.1 Grams
Fat: 18 Grams **Net Carbs:** 4.1 Grams
Ingredients:

- 1 Onion
- 1 Teaspoon Turmeric
- 7 Ounces Parmesan, Sliced
- 1 Teaspoon Sea Salt, Fine
- 1 Teaspoon Oregano
- 2 Teaspoons Butter
- 12 Ounces Beef Brisket

Directions:

1. Slice your beef into four slices, and season with oregano and turmeric.

2. Place your butter in the air fryer, and allow it to melt to coat.

3. Place your beef in next, and then add in your white onion after slicing it. Add your parmesan cheese on top, and then preheat to 365.

4. Cook for twenty-five minutes, and serve warm.

Rosemary Chicken

Serves: 12 **Time:** 1 Hour 30 Minutes
Calories: 464 **Protein:** 65.8 Grams
Fat: 20.1 Grams **Net Carbs:** 0.7 Grams
Ingredients:

- 1 Teaspoon Black Pepper
- 1 Teaspoon Sea Salt, Fine
- 6 lb. Whole Chicken
- 1 Teaspoon Paprika
- 1 Tablespoon Garlic, Minced
- 1 Teaspoon Canola Oil
- 3 tablespoons Butter
- ¼ Cup Water
- ½ Cup White Onion

Directions:

1. Rub your chicken down with salt and pepper, and then sprinkle your paprika over it. Rub your minced garlic into it, and then peel and dice your onion.
2. Placed the onion inside of your chicken, and then add your butter.
3. Rub your chicken down with canola oil, and then heat your air fryer to 360.
4. Place your chicken into your air fryer and cook for an hour and fifteen minutes. Serve warm.

Rib Eye Steak

Serves: 2 **Time:** 25 Minutes
Calories: 708 **Protein:** 40.4 Grams
Fat: 59 Grams **Net Carbs:** 1.9 Grams
Ingredients:

- 3 Tablespoons Cream
- ½ Teaspoon Chili Flakes
- 1 lb. Rib Eye Steak
- 1 Teaspoon Sea Salt, Fine
- 1 Teaspoon Cayenne pepper
- 1 Tablespoon Butter
- 1 Teaspoon Olive Oil
- 1 Teaspoon Garlic Powder
- 1 Teaspoon Lemongrass

Directions:

1. Start by heating your air fryer to 360, and then get out a shallow bowl.

2. Combine your garlic, chili flakes, salt, lemongrass and cayenne together, mixing well. Sprinkle your rib eye down with this spice mixture, and then melt your butter.

3. Combine your melted butter with our cream and olive oil. Mix well, and place this into the air fryer basket before adding in your steak.

4. Cook for thirteen minutes. Do not stir during this time. Serve warm.

Simple Pork Chops

Serves: 3
Time: 25 Minutes
Calories: 431
Protein: 27.8 Grams
Fat: 34.4 Grams
Net Carbs: 0.6 Grams
Ingredients:
- 1 Teaspoon Peppercorns
- 1 Teaspoon Sea Salt, Fine
- 1 Teaspoon Garlic, Minced
- ½ Teaspoon Rosemary
- 13 Ounces Pork Chops
- 1 Tablespoon Butter

Directions:
1. Rub your pork chops down with your spices, and then heat your air fryer to 365. Place your butter and peppercorns in your basket, and allow your butter to melt.

2. Place your pork chops in once our butter has melted, and then cook for six minutes.

3. Flip your pork chops, and then cook them for five more minutes before serving warm.

Shredded Herb Beef

Serves: 8
Time: 37 Minutes
Calories: 265
Protein: 32.4 Grams
Fat: 14 Grams
Net Carbs: 1 Gram
Ingredients:

- 4 Cups Chicken Stock
- 2 lbs. Beef Steak
- 1 Teaspoon Dill
- 1 Teaspoon Mustard
- 1 Teaspoon Sea Salt, Fine
- 1 Teaspoon Black Pepper
- 1 Teaspoon Thyme
- 1 Clove Garlic, Peeled
- 3 Tablespoons Butter
- 1 Bay Leaf

Directions:

1. Start by heating your air fryer to 360.
2. Combine all of your seasoning and mustard in a small bowl.
3. Sprinkle your beefsteak with this mixture on both sides, and allow it to soak in the spices.
4. Pour your chicken stock into your air fryer, and then add in your steak and bay leaf.
5. Cook for twenty minutes, and then strain your chicken stock, discarding the beef steak from your air fryer so you can shred it.
6. Return it back to the air fryer, and then add in your butter. Cook for two more minutes at 365, and then mix well before serving.

Pork Ribs

Serves: 5 **Time:** 1 Hour
Calories: 265 **Protein:** 24.5 Grams
Fat: 17.4 Grams **Net Carbs:** 0.7 Grams
Ingredients:
- 1 Teaspoon Garlic, Minced
- 1 Teaspoon Cayenne Pepper
- 1 Tablespoon Apple Cider Vinegar
- 1 Teaspoon Mustard
- 16 Ounces Pork Ribs
- 1 Teaspoon Chili Flakes
- 1 Teaspoon Sesame Oil
- 1 Tablespoon Paprika
- 1 Teaspoon Sea Salt, Fine

Directions:
1. Chop your ribs roughly, sprinkling them with apple cider vinegar, cayenne pepper, garlic, chili flakes and mustard.
2. Add your sesame oil and salt in, and then mix your paprika over it too.
3. Allow them to marinate in the fridge of twenty minutes.
4. Heat your air fryer to 360, and then place your pork ribs into the basket, cooking for fifteen minutes.
5. Turn your pork ribs, cooking for another fifteen minutes.
6. Serve warm.

Cheesy Drumsticks

Serves: 4
Time: 32 Minutes
Calories: 226
Protein: 16.4 Grams
Fat: 9.8 Grams
Net Carbs: 0.7 Grams
Ingredients:

- 6 Ounces Cheddar Cheese, Slice
- 1 lb. Chicken Drumsticks
- 1 Teaspoon Oregano
- 1 Teaspoon Rosemary
- ½ Teaspoon Sea Salt, Fine
- ½ Teaspoon Chili Flakes

Directions:

1. Get out your drumsticks and sprinkle with oregano, salt, rosemary and chili flakes.

2. Allow them to marinate for five minutes, and then preheat your air fryer to 370.

3. Add your drum sticks to the air fryer, cooking for ten minutes.

4. Turn your chicken to the other side, and then layer your sliced cheese on top, cooking for another three minutes.

5. Serve warm.

Garlic Chicken

Serves: 4
Time: 36 Minutes
Calories: 187
Protein: 20 Grams
Fat: 11.4 Grams
Net Carbs: 2.6 Grams
Ingredients:

- ½ Teaspoon Sea Salt, Fine
- 3 Ounces Coriander Root, Fresh
- 1 Teaspoon Olive Oil
- 3 Tablespoons Garlic, Minced
- ¼ Lemon, Sliced
- 1 Teaspoon Black Pepper
- ½ Teaspoon Chili Flakes
- 1 lb. Chicken Thighs
- 1 Tablespoon Parsley

Directions:

1. Peel your coriander root and then grate it.
2. Mix over your chicken thighs.
3. Add in your lemon and coriander root, mixing your chicken carefully. Allow the mixture to marinate for ten minutes in the fridge.

4. Preheat your air fryer to 365, and then cook for fifteen minutes.
5. Turn gently, and cook for a minute more. Serve warm.

Side Dish Recipes

Some of the recipes in the previous chapter require that you have a side dish, but luckily you can cook that in your air fryer too.

Green Bean Casserole

Serves: 8 **Time:** 25 Minutes
Calories: 201 **Protein:** 14 Grams
Fat: 15.3 Grams **Net Carbs:** 2.4 Grams
Ingredients:

- ½ Teaspoon Cayenne Pepper
- 1 Teaspoon Paprika
- 1 Teaspoon Sea Salt, Fine
- 1 Zucchini
- ¼ Cup Heavy Cream
- 6 Ounces Cheddar Cheese, Shredded
- 7 Ounces Parmesan Cheese, Shredded
- 1 Cup Green Beans
- 1 Tablespoon Parsley
- 1 Tablespoon Butter

Directions:

1. Start by cubing your zucchini, and sprinkling them down with salt and paprika.

2. Place your butter in your air fryer basket, and then add in your zucchini. Preheat your air fryer to 400, cooking for six minutes.

3. Add in your green beans, cheddar cheese and cayenne pepper next. Sprinkle your parmesan over your casserole, and then pour in your heavy cream.

4. Cook for six minutes, and then allow it to cool and chill before serving.

Spicy Asparagus

Serves: 6 **Time:** 15 Minutes
Calories: 42 **Protein:** 1.9 Grams
Fat: 2.7 Grams **Net Carbs:** 1.4 Grams
Ingredients:
- 1 Tablespoon Sesame Oil
- 1 Tablespoon Flax Seeds
- 1 lb. Asparagus
- 1 Teaspoon Sea Salt, Fine
- ½ Teaspoon White Pepper
- 1 Teaspoon Chili Flakes

Directions:
1. Combine your salt, sesame oil, white pepper and chili flakes together. Mix well.

2. Heat your air fryer to 400, and then coat it with your sesame oil mixture, and cook your asparagus for six minutes. Allow to cool before serving.

Cabbage Steaks

Serves: 4 **Time:** 15 Minutes
Calories: 37 **Protein:** 0.9 Grams
Fat: 2.3 Grams **Net Carbs:** 2.3 Grams
Ingredients:
- 9 Ounces Cabbage, Sliced
- 1 Teaspoon Sea Salt, Fine
- 1 Teaspoon Olive Oil
- 1 Teaspoon Butter
- 1 Teaspoon Paprika
- ½ Teaspoon Black Pepper

Directions:
1. Start by combining your olive oil and paprika together. Make sure to melt it, and then rub your cabbage down with it. Sprinkle with salt and pepper, and then preheat your air fryer to 400.
2. Place your cabbage in your air fryer rack, cooking for three minutes.
3. Turn them over, cooking for another two minutes.

Spicy Broccoli

Serves: 5 **Time:** 18 Minutes
Calories: 61 **Protein:** 2.7 Grams
Fat: 3.3 Grams **Net Carbs:** 4.1 Grams
Ingredients:
- 1 Teaspoon Sriracha
- 1 Tablespoon Canola Oil
- 1 Teaspoon Flax Seeds
- 1 Teaspoon White Pepper
- 1 Teaspoon Sea Salt, Fine
- 4 Tablespoons Chicken Stock
- 1 lb. Broccoli

Directions:
1. Chop your broccoli into florets.
2. Combine your Sriracha, flax seeds, white pepper and chicken stock. Add in your canola, and whisk well.
3. Preheat your air fryer to 400, and then place your broccoli in the basket rack. Sprinkle with your Sriracha mixture, and then cook for six minutes. Shake gently before serving.

Zucchini Gratin

Serves: 6 **Time:** 30 Minutes
Calories: 98 **Protein:** 8.6 Grams
Fat: 6 Grams **Net Carbs:** 2.9 Grams
Ingredients:

- 2 Zucchini
- 1 Teaspoon Black Pepper
- 1 Tablespoon Coconut Flour
- 1 Tablespoon Parsley
- 1 Teaspoon Butter
- 5 Ounces Parmesan Cheese, Shredded

Directions:

1. Combine your coconut flour, black pepper and cheese in a bowl. Shake well, and then slice your zucchini. Cut your zucchini into squares, and then spread them out in the air fryer. Heat your air fryer to 400, and mix everything together, cooking for thirteen minutes.

Kale Mash

Serves: 7
Time: 25 Minutes
Calories: 180
Protein: 10.9 Grams
Fat: 13.2 Grams
Net Carbs: 5.1 Grams
Ingredients:

- 1 lb. Italian Dark Leaf Kale
- 7 Ounces Parmesan, Shredded
- 1 Cup Heavy Cream
- 1 Teaspoon Sea Salt, Fine
- 1 Teaspoon Butter
- 1 Teaspoon Black Pepper
- 1 Onion, Diced

Directions:

1. Chop the kale, adding it into your air fryer basket. Sprinkle in your remaining ingredients, and then heat your air fryer to 250.

2. Cook for twelve minutes, and then mix well before serving.

Spicy Creamed Mushrooms

Serves; 4 **Time:** 25 Minutes
Calories: 84
Protein: 2.9 Grams
Fat: 2.9 Grams
Net Carbs: 5.6 Grams
Ingredients:

- 1 Teaspoon Butter
- 1 Teaspoon Olive Oil
- 1 Onion, Sliced
- 1 Cup Cream
- 1 Teaspoon Garlic, Sliced
- 9 Ounces White mushrooms
- 1 Teaspoon Red Pepper, Ground
- 1 Teaspoon Chili Flakes

Directions:

1. Start by slicing your mushrooms, and then sprinkle them with red pepper and chili flakes. Make sure to mix well, and then preheat your air fryer to 400.

2. Oil your air fryer basket with olive oil, adding in your mushrooms. Cook for five minutes, and then add in your remaining ingredients. Decrease the temperature to 365, and cook for seven more minutes. Stir well before serving.

Squash Spaghetti

Serves: 8

Time: 20 Minutes

Calories: 55

Protein: 0.7 Grams

Fat: 3.4 Grams

Net carbs: 5.5 Grams

Ingredients:

- 1 lb. Winter Squash
- 1 Cup Chicken Stock
- 4 Tablespoons Heavy Cream
- 1 Teaspoon Sea Salt, Fine
- 1 Teaspoon Black Pepper
- 1 Teaspoon Butter

Directions:

1. Start by peeling and grating your winter squash, and then heat your air fryer to 400 place it in your basket, covering with chicken stock and seasoning with salt and pepper. Cook for ten minutes.

2. Strain the liquid, and then add in your butter and heavy cream. Serve warm.

Dessert Recipes

Ketogenic friendly desserts become a piece of cake when you're using an air fryer. Indulge your sweet tooth easily and healthily with these dessert recipes.

Peanut Butter "Cookies"

Serves: 8

Time: 25 Minutes

Calories: 102

Protein: 4.7 Grams

Fat: 8.6 Grams

Net Carbs: 9.7 Grams

Ingredients:

- 4 Tablespoons Erythritol
- 8 Tablespoons Peanut Butter
- ¼ Teaspoon Sea Salt, Fine
- 1 Egg

Directions:
1. Get out a big bowl and mix all of your ingredients together except for your egg.
2. Crack your egg, and then add it into your mixture, mixing until it makes a dough.
3. Roll it out using a rolling pin, and then cut with a cookie cutter.
4. Make a cross pattern with a fork on every cookie, and then heat your air fryer to 360.
5. Place them in the fryer basket, and cook for ten minutes. Allow them to cool before serving.

Poppy Balls

Serves: 11 **Time:** 30 Minutes
Calories: 83 **Protein:** 2.1 Grams
Fat: 4.9 Grams **Net Carbs:** 3.6 Grams
Ingredients:

- ½ Cup Heavy Cream
- ¼ Teaspoon Sea Salt, Fine
- 1 Cup Coconut Flour
- ½ Teaspoon Cinnamon
- 4 Tablespoons Poppy Seeds
- 1 Teaspoon Butter
- ¼ Teaspoon Ginger
- ½ Teaspoon Baking Powder
- ½ Teaspoon Apple Cider Vinegar
- 3 Tablespoons Stevia Extract

Directions:

1. Start by mixing your ginger, baking powder cinnamon, salt, flour and poppy seeds together.

2. Add in your melted butter, mixing gently.

3. Next, add in your stevia and vinegar.

4. Add your heavy cream before kneading until it turns into a soft, elastic dough.

5. Cut into eleven balls, and then heat your air fryer to 365. Place your balls in the basket, and cook for three minutes.

6. Shake them, and cook for five more minutes.

Green Pudding

Serves: 3

Time: 15 Minutes

Calories: 199

Protein: 2.2 Grams

Fat: 19.3 Grams

Net Carbs: 2.6 Grams

Ingredients:

- 5 Tablespoons Almond Milk
- ¼ Teaspoon Vanilla Extract
- ¼ Teaspoon Salt
- 3 Teaspoons Stevia Extract
- 1 Avocado, Pitted
- 1 Tablespoon Cocoa Powder

Directions:

1. Heat your oven to 360, and then peel and mash your avocado. You can do this with a fork.
2. Combine all of your ingredients together with a hand mixer, and then place it in the basket.
3. Cook for three minutes.

Vanilla Mousse

Serves: 4
Time: 25 Minutes
Calories: 228
Protein: 3.1 Grams
Fat: 23.1 Grams
Net Carbs: 2.3 Grams
Ingredients:
- 1 Teaspoon Vanilla Extract, Pure
- ½ Cup Cream Cheese
- ½ Cup Almond Milk
- 2 Teaspoons Stevia Extract
- ¼ Cup Blackberries
- 2 Tablespoons Butter
- ¼ Teaspoon Cinnamon

Directions:
1. Start by heating your air fryer to 320.
2. Combine your vanilla, almond milk, and butter mix well, and then place it in your air fryer. Cook for six minutes, and then stir. Chill until it comes to room temperature, and then place your blackberries in a bowl.
3. Mash your blackberries, and then get out a second bowl. Whisk your cream cheese for two minutes in this bowl, adding in your blackberries. Whisk for another minute, and then add in your stevia and cinnamon. Stir well, and combine your mixtures together.
4. Allow it to cool in the fridge before serving.

Sweetened Bacon Cookies

Serves: 6
Time: 20 Minutes
Calories: 109
Protein: 5.2 Grams
Fat: 8.8 Grams
Net Carbs: 3 Grams
Ingredients:

- 4 Slices Bacon, Cooked & Chopped
- ¼ Teaspoon Baking Soda
- 5 Tablespoons Peanut Butter
- 3 Tablespoons Swerve
- ¼ Teaspoon Ginger
- ½ Teaspoon Vanilla Extract

Directions:

1. Combine your baking soda, swerve, ginger, and peanut butter.

2. Add in your chopped bacon, mixing well.

3. Roll into a log, and cut it into six pieces. Flatten each one, and then heat your air fryer to 350.

4. Place your cookies in your basket, cooking for seven minutes.

5. Allow to cool before serving.

Hazelnut Balls

Serves: 8
Time: 30 Minutes
Calories: 123
Protein: 4.4 Grams
Fat: 10.1 Grams
Net Carbs: 7.9 Grams
Ingredients:

- 2 Tablespoons Peanut Butter
- 3 Tablespoons Erythritol
- ½ Teaspoon Vanilla Extract, Pure
- 1 Cup Almond Flour
- ½ Teaspoon Baking Soda
- 4 Tablespoons Hazelnuts, Crushed
- 1 Teaspoon Apple Cider Vinegar

Directions:

1. Place your peanut butter in a bowl, and add in your sweetener. Stir well, and then add in your remaining ingredients. Knead to form a soft dough, and then cut into eight pieces.

2. Roll your balls from this dough, and then heat your air fryer to 360. Cook for eight minutes, allowing them to cool before serving.

Air Fryer Blackberry Muffins

Serves: 5
Time: 25 Minutes
Calories: 165
Protein: 2 Grams
Fat: 16.4 Grams
Net Carbs: 2.1 Grams
Ingredients:

- 4 Tablespoons Butter
- 1 Cup Almond Flour
- 1 Teaspoon Apple Cider Vinegar
- 6 Tablespoons Almond Milk
- 1 Teaspoon Baking Soda
- 3 Ounces Blackberries
- ½ Teaspoon Sea Salt, Fine
- 3 Teaspoons Stevia
- 1 Teaspoon Vanilla Extract, Pure

Directions:

1. Place your almond flour in a bowl, adding in your baking soda, salt, vanilla extract and stevia
2. After this, add in your almond milk, apple cider vinegar and butter.
3. Mash your blackberries gently, adding them to the mixture.
4. Mix well, and then allow it to sit in a warm place for five minutes.
5. Preheat your air fryer to 400, and ten prepare your muffin forms.
6. Pour the dough in, making sure to only fill them halfway.

7. Add in your muffin forms, and cook for ten minutes.
8. Allow them to come to room temperature or chill before serving.

Healthy Chia Pudding

Serves: 7
Time: 15 Minutes
Calories: 204
Protein: 4.8 Grams
Fat: 16.4 Grams
Net Carbs: 2 Grams
Ingredients:

- 1 Cup Chia Seeds
- 1 Teaspoon Stevia
- 1 Cup Coconut Milk
- 1 Tablespoon Coconut
- 1 Teaspoon Butter

Directions:

1. Get out small ramekins, placing your chia seeds in.

2. Add in your milk and stevia, mixing gently but well.

3. Add in your butter and coconut.

4. Place your pudding in the air fryer after it's been heated to 360.

5. Cook for four minutes, and then allow it to chill for four minutes before serving.

Conclusion

Now you know everything you need to in order to cook healthy, delicious ketogenic meals in your air fryer. There's no reason that you should settle for less than tasty, delicious food that reminds you of the comfort food you're leaving behind. With the right food and texture, your cravings will be minimized so that you can maximize your success with the ketogenic lifestyle. Just pick a recipe to get started, and you'll be experimenting with your air fryer in no time at all! It'll easily become a kitchen staple.

27635126R00061

Made in the USA
Lexington, KY
02 January 2019